Narcissistic Abuse

22 problems emotional abuse survivors struggle with and how to overcome them and LIVE A JOYFUL LIFE

the rendering of legal, financial, medical or professional advice. The content within this book has been derived from various sources. Please consult a licensed professional before attempting any techniques outlined in this book.

By reading this document, the reader agrees that under no circumstances is the author responsible for any losses, direct or indirect, which are incurred as a result of the use of information contained within this document, including, but not limited to, — errors, omissions, or inaccuracies.

Table Of Contents

Introduction 9

Chapter One: What Is Narcissistic Abuse? 12

Symptoms of NPD 13

Types of Narcissistic Abuse 15

Types of Abuse 16

Verbal Abuse 17

Manipulation 17

Emotional Blackmail 17

Gaslighting 18

Lying 19

Withholding 20

Neglect 21

Privacy Invasion 21

Character Assassination 21

Financial Abuse 22

Isolation 22

Chapter Two: The Aftereffects of Narcissistic Abuse 25

Anxiety 27

PTSD 29

Physical Numbness *31*

Memory Loss *31*

Fight-or-Flight Response *31*

Depression 32

Sleeplessness and Loneliness 33

Tiredness 34

Frustration and Anger 36

Loss of Sex Drive 39

Trauma Bonding 40

Why Does the Narcissist Do This? *42*

The Stages of Narcissistic Trauma Bonding *45*

Intermittent Reinforcement 46

How Did You Fit the Bill? *47*

Confusion 49

Suicidal Thoughts 50

Feeling Crazy 51

Effect on the Brain 52

Have You Wondered Why Memory Loss Occurs during Abuse? *53*

How Do You Reverse the Damage Done to the Hippocampus and Amygdala? *55*

What Do You Think About This Book so Far? 57

Chapter Three: Healing from Narcissistic Abuse 58

Denial 62

Anger 62

Bargaining 64

Depression 64

Acceptance 65

How to Heal from the Narcissistic Abuse 67

What Does Building and Setting Boundaries Mean? 68

No Contact 71

The Breaking of No Contact 74

How to Implement No Contact When Children Are Involved? 78

Parental Alienation 80

How to Co-Parent with a Narcissist.................. 84

Maintain Documentation 84

Do Not Criticize the Narcissist in Front of the Children...86

Triangulation 86

Educate Your Kids...87

Seek a Parent Coordinator through the Court... 87

Have a Guardian for the Children 88

Refuse to Make Your Child a Pawn........................ 88

Have a Detailed Custody Agreement.................. 89

Child Counseling.. 89

Manage Your Expectations 89

Still in Love with the Abuser? 90

You Remember Only the "Good" Times 91

You Remember the Narcissist's Traumatic Past 92

Savior Complex 93

Love Could Be a Survival Technique for You..... 94

Codependency 95

Chapter Four: When to Start Dating Again? 99

Paranoid that Everyone Is a Narcissist............. 99

Tips to Begin Dating 101

Chapter Five: Spiritual Healing after the Narcissistic Abuse 105

Why Must You Forgive Yourself?.....................107

Chapter Six: Four Pillars for Recovery from Narcissistic Abuse 116

Self-Esteem.. 118

Self-Worth 118

Self-Trust 120

Self-Love 121

How Long Does It Take to Heal Completely? .123

Conclusion 126

References.................................... 130

Introduction

How many times have you heard the quote "Love heals everything" or "Love is the only hope in life" or something similar to those lines?

When you look around you, you see all these people happily in love and singing poems about the wonders of love. And then you are confused why you are not able to feel anything on those lines. All you feel is a pit in your stomach, a sense of fear and of always being on edge, but all you did was love, right? You did or are doing everything right, yet this "love" does not seem to be magical or does not seem to be healing you; rather, it appears to be destroying you by driving you crazy, and you notice that you have changed not for good.

My first book on Narcissistic abuse was published in October 2018, and I started writing it, just to share what had helped me after I left my husband after 10 years of emotional abuse. I had been researching a lot on the subject and found some great books online however I just wanted to share the scriptures and prayer plan that had helped me and a few women in my close circle, to get over our terrible experiences. Even though I had been divorced for 3 years at the time I wrote the book, I didn't feel ready to share my personal story. In this book, I will share parts of my story, not because I want to prove a point of how much I suffered, but I realize that survivors of psychological abuse share the same fears, and the purpose of my writing this book, is to hold your hand and give you the courage to face yours as I still do every single day to this very day.

I am assuming that if you have arrived here reading this book, then you have already begun the journey of true healing and magic. God has directed our paths to cross at this moment in time and I feel privileged to help guide you in the right direction to find true healing and peace.

Love, for sure, heals and is magical but only when done in the right manner. In the name of love, people can be poisonous and damage even the strongest souls. It is for this reason that love with a narcissist is bad because it is the wrong type of love. A narcissist does not understand love the way normal people understand it.

Narcissistic abuse is high on the ranks of toxic forms of love. It damages and destroys the soul like no other, completely changing the way you look at yourself. It rips your soul apart and causes destruction. And that is the biggest danger because no matter how the world looks at you, once your idea of yourself changes, then the damage is done.

In this book, you will be taken on a journey of healing by understanding the various forms of abuse, the ways to heal, and finally, the ways to find closure.

If you are not the victim who is reading this but know someone who may be in the situation, then this book will help you empathize with the victim and help them deal with their situation.

Congratulations on taking the first step toward healing: accepting the problem. As it has been said, "to err is human, to forgive is divine," by the time you finish this book, you will be able to forgive yourself and attain closure.

God bless.

Chapter One: What Is Narcissistic Abuse?

Before going on to understand narcissistic abuse, it is helpful to know

- who is a narcissist
- what qualifies as narcissistic abuse

A narcissistic person is someone with an excessive interest or admiration of himself or herself to the point of self-worship. Narcissism denotes a person with an exaggerated sense of self. He or she is so convinced of his or her sense of self that they expect everyone around them also to worship them.

Scientifically speaking, a narcissist is a person who has a narcissist personality disorder, also known as NPD, as defined in the *Diagnostic and Statistical Manual of Mental Disorders* (DSM).

Grandiosity is the hallmark of a narcissist followed by lack of empathy and a constant severe need for admiration and control. People suffering from this disorder believe that they are superior to the rest of the world and hence the need for superior treatment and appreciation.

This enhances their self-esteem, which in reality is very fragile. They also have extreme difficulty tolerating any form of criticism and rejection because this damages their self-esteem and makes them feel humiliated and defeated which they cannot accept.

Symptoms of NPD

- Exaggerates own importance
- Is constantly preoccupied with fantasies of success, power, beauty, romance, and power
- Requires constant admiration
- Has unreasonable expectations of superior treatment than others
- Manipulative and uses others to reach or attain their goals
- Complete disregard for the feelings of others
- Envy and jealousy are their core traits
- Arrogant and often disrespectful of boundaries

A narcissist, in reality, has a very shallow self-image and it is this low self-image that they try to offset by idealizing themselves. A narcissist has convinced himself that he is the greatest, and it is this greatness that they want everyone to accept and admire. Deep down, they feel shame for all this gap and the facade they have created but have too big of an ego to accept the shame. They work day and night to avoid feeling shame. To fill this gap, they resort to destructive mechanisms, and hence, their behavior becomes abuse and is called "narcissistic abuse."

They turn to abusive behaviors as a form of self-defense because they cannot see themselves fall. It is often the loved ones who become victims of their abuse, as it is only loved ones that they have absolute control over. So the whole world can see them as an angel but only those are close enough know who they truly are.

If you remember in the introduction, I mention how love is supposed to be healing. A narcissist, though incapable of loving someone other than their self, completely understands that love can be used to control others. Hence, the victims of narcissistic abuse are always immediate family and friends whom the narcissist has completely managed to manipulate.

A narcissist is extremely intelligent and knows the various ways to get his way and effectively uses them in the hope that the victim never finds out the truth.

A narcissist's ultimate fear is a victim finding out the truth because this indicates that the abuse and control cannot be continued if the victim becomes strong. Hence, a narcissist will do everything in his hands to keep the victim isolated and manipulate the victim into believing that the problem lies with the victim and not with himself thereby creating confusion.

In the next chapters, I would talk about different methods of abuse, the effects of narcissistic abuse, and finally, the healing methods.

Types of Narcissistic Abuse

The biggest problem with the narcissistic form of abuse is that especially in the beginning stages it all seems strange and weird, but it does not seem or look like abuse.

Last but not the least, most narcissists seldom show their true side to the world, and this includes anyone in your common circle, and hence, even when you know you are being abused, there is no one you can confide in because *no one* is ever going to believe you. It could also be possible that the one or two times you showed courage and tried to tell or explain how you felt to friends or family, they would have dismissed you stating that you are exaggerating things, and people will not believe you or give you the validation that you need. This is exactly why it is important to understand that *you* are not wrong in how you feel; it is just that you need to understand the symptoms of the abuse.

A narcissist manages to convince the whole world about their goodness because they are charmers, suave in their approach, and extremely intelligent and guarded about their moves. Remember that it is because of all this that you would have fallen for them in the first place.

Types of Abuse

The first and most obvious thing that comes to mind when abuse is discussed is physical abuse. Sadly, a lot of people believe that if there is no beating involved, then it is not abuse. Abuse comes in several forms. It can be emotional, mental, financial, and sexual. Here are a few examples of abuse:

Verbal Abuse

This need not necessarily mean shouting at the top of the voice, but it can involve bullying, being critical of everything, blaming, shaming, name calling, sarcasm, and rage. For the narcissist, this is not something that happens once in a while, it is a pattern that they intentionally use to manipulate and gain control over people. Some times, verbal abuse can be in the form of a joke, where they do or say things intentionally to irritate you, and when it does, they say 'It was just a joke', and might blame you again for being too sensitive.

Manipulation

Manipulation means the indirect influence on another person to behave in a manner that serves the purpose of the manipulator. Manipulation can initially be very difficult to spot because on the surface everything seems all right and you seem to even agree with the manipulator, but deep down, the manipulator is controlling the situation by making you do what he wants to. Slowly you start feeling low and sense a hostile intent.

Emotional Blackmail

This may include threats, anger warnings, intimidation, or punishment. You will never know what will cause the person to show these negative emotions. You constantly feel fear, obligation and guilt (*FOG*). Everything starts appearing hazy to you, and you lose the sense of the actual situation. They behave inappropriately then blame their own actions on you. A typical example of this happens when the narcissist is caught cheating, and instead of feeling remorseful, they turn around and blame their partner for not being around, or working too much and neglecting their needs. Emotional blackmail is a powerful form of manipulation, some toxic people threats to harm themselves as a tactic to gain control over their victim.

Gaslighting

This is a term associated with psychological abuse, it happens when an abusive partner manipulates their victim by psychological means to the point of them questioning their own sanity. They deny and twist reality so smoothly, they try to make you believe their own version of reality which is usually totally fabricated. Their intent is to do whatever they want and get away with it, and they succeed at this by getting you confused, vulnerable and weak. In most cases, the goal of the abuser is to make their victim so unsure of their ability to make decisions or trust their emotions so much that they have to depend on their abuser.

My ex husband was very subtle with his Gaslighting; it took me years to even understand what was going on. He tried to convince me that things I had not memory of had happened. It started with minor things like he would make up things I had said in previous conversations that I knew were totally out of character for me to say. Then it got worse to the point where my things started disappearing and even though he knew exactly what I was looking for he would try to persuade me that the item never existed. He told me constantly that I was insane and blamed me for not doing things he never asked me to do. Thankfully I eventually caught on and started keeping detailed journals and writing important information, that helped me remember.

This is one of the biggest indicators of abuse. In this case, you are made to distrust your close friends, family, or anyone whom you trust. The abuser tries all the tricks possible to make you distrust perception of reality.

Lying

Persistent lying to achieve the narcissist's own goals. Infidelity is something very common amongst narcissist. They lie to hide infidelity, they lie to blame everything on you, and they lie to others about you. They lie to others about how intelligent or skillful they are. They think of themselves as gods, so they don't feel responsible to explain their actions to anyone. During the love bombing stage at the beginning of a relationship, they lie about being caring and considerate, only to pull you in before the abuse begins. Being with a narcissist for long, some people are able to call them out on this behavior, but that usually leads no where because they turn always find a way to turn the blame on you.

Withholding

This can include withholding sex, money, communication, and affection from you. This can also include giving you the "silent treatment," wherein they stop communicating with you or ignore for anything that disturbs them. They refuse to engage the other person in any meaningful contact. My ex husband would decide not to speak with me for weeks just because he accused me of doing something, even when I apologized, all I would get from him anytime I tried to engage him in a conversation where one liners. He would say things like 'I'm off to work' after ignoring me for the entire day.

Neglect

This means ignoring your needs or the needs of any children you have together. They sometimes completely abandon their household responsibilities. They care about no one but themselves, so even an infant can be affected by their neglect, and it wouldn't make a difference. If something does not directly benefit them, they don't show any interest whatsoever.

Privacy Invasion

A narcissist has no respect for boundaries. He will constantly be checking on you, stalking you, checking our phone and email, and ignoring any privacy you have requested. It is mind boggling especially when you know that they are the ones being unfaithful.

Character Assassination

They slander you by spreading malicious gossip about you and try to destroy your image at work and among friends and family. They are able to do this because people outside see them as kind, respectful individuals. This is why victims usually refer to narcissist as wearing mask. They are great actors and they would use any means to maintain control over their victims.

Financial Abuse

Financial abuse may also include controlling you through economic domination or draining of your finances by accruing debt on your name, extortion, or selling your personal property.

Isolation

The narcissist's first step is isolation because, without isolation, it is difficult to achieve all their goals. The narcissist will ensure that you lose all your friends, family members, and even acquaintances. This they achieve through control, manipulation, verbal abuse, character assassination, and other means.

Narcissism and the extent to which the above behaviors are displayed vary from time to time and intensity. The narcissist works on the strategy to make things unpredictable for you. Narcissistic abuse transforms a hopeful, positive person into someone constantly in doubt, always looking over the shoulder—worried, a person who has no confidence.

By now you must have gotten a fair idea about the

types of abuse and how the narcissist works. It can be very heartbreaking to understand that you have been through something so harmful and that this harmful behavior was by a person whom you loved and gave your everything.

Accepting that you have undergone abuse is the first step in healing. Do not blame yourself for what you have gone through. Apart from accepting the abuse, another important factor is to acknowledge that you did not invite this upon yourself. *You* are not at fault for anything that you were subjected to. One common feeling amongst survivors is guilt.

The first step in the healing journey is to forgive yourself. Trust in God, and you will be able to forgive yourself eventually. The ultimate goal is to be able to attain closure by forgiving yourself and moving on in your life.

Remember this: forgiveness does not mean going back to old ways; it simply means acknowledging all that has happened to be for your good and proceeding ahead with faith and confidence.

This is also the time when you may have noticed that no matter whom you confide in, nobody seems to understand you. This is because just like you, everyone is trapped by the false image, so do not blame others if they do not understand you.

You can try explaining it to them by giving them an example that they can relate to. For example, tell them about how if their laptop gets a virus, would they still expect it to function in the same manner? Or if there is an underlying illness, then it takes time for the symptoms to show up fully, but at the end of the day, you need to accept that people may not fully understand you for a very long time.

In the next few chapters, I would take you through the after effects of facing abuse and how you can overcome them.

Chapter Two: The Aftereffects of Narcissistic Abuse

There are several after effects to narcissistic abuse. Most of them start during the relationship phase because even before you identify the problem, your body and mind recognize that something is not right and start exhibiting symptoms from the abuse. Abuse alters the way you think by entirely changing your perspective because you are no longer under your control but under the control of the abuser.

You may be wondering whether you are going mad or turning into a crazy person as the effects of the abuse lingers on long after the abuse has ended. Please understand that this is *normal.*

You are not going crazy, but it is your body and mind's way of dealing with the abuse that is inflicted upon. Hence, despite cutting off the relationship, healing takes time and a lot of patience.

During the healing journey, it is extremely important that you are *kind* and *compassionate* to yourself. Do not be critical of yourself and expect results overnight.

You may be wondering how long it will take? Well, the answer is that nobody knows how long it will take. While the relationship might have been for a short period, the healing takes a very long time. It also varies from person to person, so it is beneficial if you do not compare yourself to others and feel demotivated.

Faith in God also helps during this time. A lot of times, some people stop having faith in God or angry with God for subjecting them to this kind of torture. It is very common to question your faith, and if you are one of those, then do not feel guilty for feeling this way. Simply put, your mind wants to process all that has happened and hence will go through various phases. This is also a passing phase. It will pass, and you will soon find out that God has never left you alone. Throughout your battle, God gave you the required strength by bringing you in touch with the right kind of resources and people to help you heal. The world is an imperfect place, with imperfect people and for me I found that leaning on God helped me to stay grounded through my experience.

Brace yourself for the journey and continue reading to find out about the various effects of abuse and how to heal from it.

Anxiety

The stressful experiences victims are subjected to, often leads to anxiety, as the body naturally responds to stress that way. A constant feeling of fear of the unknown, the mind is in a perpetual state of panic as a way to defend itself, by forcing the person to flee that environment.

Anxiety happens when you live anywhere close to abuse. This can be due to mental, emotional, physical, or any abuse. This is because, in a relationship with a narcissist, you are constantly being put down and are being told that *you* are the cause of all troubles. Anxiety also happens in some cases because every time you summon the courage to report the abuse or confront the abuser, you are told that you are overreacting. Therefore, the brain does not understand how to handle all this, and thus, you have anxiety. Fear and anxiety are normal emotions everyone goes through at one point of the other, but when it never goes away and even gets worse with time, to the point where it starts to interfere with your day to day activities, you might be suffering from an anxiety disorder.

Anxiety may also cause you to experience panic attacks or panic disorders. These attacks lead to repeated episodes of intense anxiety. A narcissist manages to convince the whole world about their goodness because they are charmers, suave in their approach and extremely intelligent and guarded about their moves.

You may develop social anxiety, which involves high levels of anxiety, fear, and complete avoidance of social gatherings because of feelings of embarrassment and concern about being judged by others.

The first sign of your relationship with a narcissist is when you start feeling anxious for no specific reason. You start feeling trapped and begin to identify that something is wrong with your situation; however, the constant claims that the narcissist makes about your irrational behavior make you question yourself, and thus, you are lost and you develop anxiety.

Anxiety develops first because the brain is wired to respond to unhealthy behaviors. It is an evolutionary response to that is supposed to help you detect dangers and deal with those dangers.

In a way, the brain is telling you that something is wrong and that you have to make the wrong right.

So do not worry about the anxiety or panic attacks. It means that your body has identified threats and now you need to make things right.

PTSD

Post-traumatic stress disorder (PTSD) usually develops after the trauma of any kind. It is seen is army personnel who have served in wars to people who were involved in accidents to people like *you* who were abused.

If you have suffered from narcissistic abuse, it is common to experience constant flashbacks, almost like you are re-experiencing the entire trauma again. This can be very painful to deal with. Memories of trauma are involuntarily recalled despite you trying very hard not to recall them. This is because the memories are associated with trauma and can be caused by anything in the environment that resembles the event when the actual trauma occurred. The intrusive memories are extremely clear, making you feel like you are experiencing it all over again. You experience extreme fear because you feel like you are reliving the trauma.

These flashbacks are unique to PTSD, and these can also occur in the form of nightmares and cause tremendous fear in you. The nightmares are usually threatening or frightening dreams that awaken you and are followed by an intense negative emotion such as anger, fear, or sadness. You may experience body pains and muscle aches when you get up from your dream suddenly and find yourself often breaking down, unable to handle the emotional turmoil.

This is because unlike regular nightmares that you may experience, post-trauma nightmares are exceptionally intense as they contain the exact replay of the events that happened. These are called as replicative nightmares, where the dream plays out exactly the way it happened in real life, and you end up feeling like it is happening all over again and become helpless.

Flashback is also common where you may catch yourself during the day reliving those memories from the past. It is these intrusive thoughts and memories that lead to stress.

In some cases, these replicative dreams may persist even decades after the trauma has happened.

Apart from the above most common sign of PTSD, below are some other signs:

Physical Numbness

This can be anywhere in the body, right from toes, lips, muscles, etc., to emotional numbness (i.e., the inability to feel any emotion, especially unable to find joy in things that would otherwise bring joy to a normal person).

Memory Loss

You may be wondering how you remember and get nightmares about the abuse but tend to have forgotten a lot of other things. You cannot recollect certain parts of your life no matter how hard you try.

Fight-or-Flight Response

Your body is constantly on alert, and the slightest feeling of threat can send you into a fight or flight mode which means that either you are angry and want to fight or you want to escape.

PTSD happens because when you are exposed to narcissistic abuse, you are trapped, and your inner being is ripped apart. This is almost similar to living in a war zone.

The good news is that there is help around. You can seek help by consulting psychologists who are trained in this.

Depression

It is a very well-known fact that a breakup with a narcissist and even a relationship with a narcissist is extremely painful. Pain circuit within your brain is activated during this time. This feeling offsets your emotions, and you begin questioning everything. All this questioning leads to "Why me?"

When you start questioning "Why me?" you tend to become angry and upset that you were cheated and betrayed. This can lead you to think that you must have done something wrong or that you were unworthy of a good relationship. All these negative emotions can lead to low self-esteem and eventually to depression.

A narcissist thrives on making you lose your self-esteem and wants to tear you apart because only that will make them feel good. They will put in a lot of effort to ensure that this happens. Hence, when you understand this background, it is only natural that you expect an apology.

An apology never happens, and if it happens, it is never true. Even here your expectations are not met, and you go down the negative road. All this leads to depression simply because of the helplessness, betrayal, and the cheating you have experienced.

The fear that you are crazy can make depression worse. Depressive episodes usually peak as soon as you get up in the morning and open your eyes. It does not matter that you have still not gotten out of bed, but you already feel a lump in your throat and sometimes can even break down immediately.

Sleeplessness and Loneliness

All the nightmares and terrors make a seemingly easy task like sleeping seem like conquering the Mount Everest. It becomes impossible to catch even a few hours of sleep because no sooner do you close your eyes, you are bombarded with nightmares and traumatic feelings. Despite the constant fatigue, sleep eludes you. Depression adds to the woes by making it even worse. Feelings of loneliness and vulnerability are heightened at night and ensure that you do not sleep.

All the negative emotions and lack of self-esteem followed by social anxiety can make you want to avoid any social setting, thus making you prone to loneliness, even during the day.

Loneliness is also present because the narcissist would have cleverly isolated you from any human being he perceives as a threat or thinks will support you. It is extremely common for victims of narcissistic abuse to have lost all friends and contact with even close family members because that is just how the narcissist works. The narcissist would have enjoyed that you cut off the relations with everyone so now when you need any form of support you are left with none. All these feelings can worsen the depressive episodes.

Tiredness

If you're drowning in the aftermath of the narcissistic abuse, you will soon realize that you feel older than your age and generally exhausted.

Your muscles become stiff, you constantly feel tired and overwhelmed, and your joints are always in pain. This is because living with a narcissist is like living inside a volcano; you never know when he will explode. All the constant stress weakens your system because there is only so much stress the human body can handle. No matter how strong you are, there comes a crumbling time when your body gives up. It begins to stop cooperating, and that is when all these symptoms show up.

Exposure to constant abuse transforms your body into a state of fight or flight. When your body is in a state of fight or flight, its natural response is to produce cortisol. Cortisol is a hormone that is produced by the body when it is under extreme duress. When you are stressed, the amount of cortisol increases as your body has to manage increased levels of stress. Over some time, your body cannot deal with the stress anymore, and this is when you start feeling exhausted and tired all the time. A narcissist destroys both your body and mind at the same time.

Narcissistic abuse is difficult to spot initially because a narcissist is rarely overt, especially in the initial days. The abuse is silent and subdued, and because of which, you fail to recognize it. A narcissist will rarely indulge in physical abuse, and this makes things all the more difficult for you to process because you and society, in general, are conditioned to believe that if there are no bruises, then there is no abuse.

You are stressed because of both the abuse as well as trying to make sense of the extreme highs and lows in your relationship. All this stress starts showing up as soon as the stressor (i.e., the narcissist is removed from your life). Your body senses that the threat is no longer there and starts relaxing. This is when you begin processing all that has happened to you and experience nightmares and flashbacks.

Exposure to abuse causes this kind of adrenal fatigue because the primary function of the adrenal glands is to help deal with stress. Hence, during your relationship with the narcissist, your adrenal glands are working overtime beyond their capacity to help you deal with the stress and trauma that is being inflicted on you. Now with the abuser gone, the stressor is removed, and hence, you have fatigue. This is made worse by the fact that you are suffering from sleeplessness and depression. The constant nightmares keep you awake all night, and this, in turn, causes fatigue.

Frustration and Anger

Feeling frustrated after narcissistic abuse is natural because when you are away from the abuser and have attained clarity about the abuse, you feel frustrated that you let it happen to you.

All through the abuse, you must have learned to cope with it by disassociating yourself from the situation and hence never understood the depth of the abuse. This is because to survive the situation, your body tries to disassociate itself. While in the situation, you would not have allowed the impact of the abuse to affect you and stay in your consciousness, but the brain would have internalized it all. Once you are not dealing with the abuse and the abuser on a day-to-day basis, the most common reaction to being violated, anger, will rise.

Anger is a self-protective mechanism that is present in your body to guard your body against threats. Hence, feeling the anger will help you will help you progress from feeling helpless to feeling empowered at facing the violation. It will slowly help you transition from feeling like a victim to a survivor and thus like a winner.

Also, understand that this anger is "right anger," right because it is entirely your right as a normal human being to feel anger for being violated at all levels, your right for being cheated and used for the abuser's benefit, and ultimately, your right to give yourself the respect you deserve.

You feel all this anger only because your soul was torn apart by the person whom you showered all the love with, and hence, it is very natural, and you must let your body feel it by acknowledging it.

Feeling anger is empowering and a step in the right direction. In the past, you were forced to suppress the natural anger that could have protected you with many consequences to your emotional, physical, and spiritual well-being. Do not commit the mistake of suppressing the anger you are experiencing right now. Experience it fully and feel it all through.

Your body and mind should fully understand the violation to defend you from someone who crosses the boundaries, who is abusive or controlling.

This is also why exercise is recommended during the process, as it will help channelize all the anger. Expending the energy via exercises that are vigorous—or something like drumming, journaling, kickboxing, screaming, verbal expression, or other techniques through which you can release your anger—will help you give it the importance it deserves and thus deal with it.

Once you fully feel the impact of the violation that happened to you, it will eventually give way to learning about yourself and also the dark human nature and how to go forward from here in a safe, protected way. Forgiveness or denial is never the antidote to the abuse you have experienced at the hands of the abuser; rather, facing the anger with complete acceptance is the only way to move forward. Once you accept, you will derive the strength that is required to heal.

Once this anger has been fully acknowledged and given due importance, you will be amazed that it will leave you. It will leave you to live your own life and move forward and will not come back.

So the good news is that this anger does not stay long within your system. It will stay as long as you allow it to stay by not dealing with it.

Deal with it and let it go.

Loss of Sex Drive

You may experience a loss in sex drive post the breakup with a narcissist. This happens because the narcissist whom you were in a relationship with may have used sex as a weapon to manipulate you.

A sexual narcissist is one who has an inflated sense of his sexual prowess and uses sex to control and manipulate the victim. A sexual narcissist rarely gets intimate on an emotional level, and sex with him is almost always a competition with him focused on his performance and constantly seeking validation. A sexual narcissist forces you to engage in acts that you are not comfortable in by manipulating you. Genuine human emotions are missing in lovemaking because the narcissist uses you as a tool. In the mind of a narcissist, you exist only to serve him at his beck and call. You will only be used as a tool for his pleasure and satisfaction.

This lack of emotion during lovemaking and not paying attention to your feelings can make something otherwise pleasurable like sex also seem like a task. This is also because the narcissist is only concerned about satisfying himself and does not bother about you, which leads to a loss in sex drive.

Trauma Bonding

Trauma bonding is one of the most dangerous effects of narcissistic abuse. Have you ever felt this intense longing to go back to your abuser? You may be wondering if you are crazy that you are craving the abuser. If you answer yes, then you are experiencing trauma bonding.

Trauma bonding is a strong emotional attachment to the abuser as a result of the ill-treatment. Simply put, it is craving for the abuser and abuse. Trauma bonding makes you crave the abuser, and then when you regain your senses briefly, you wonder why in the first place you were craving the abuse back in your life.

Trauma bonding happens because of continuous cycles of abuse from intermittent usage of reward and punishment, and this cycle creates emotional bonds that are extremely difficult to break.

Traumatic bonding appears in relationships such as the one with a narcissist. One reason trauma bond occurs between a normal person who is the victim and an abnormal person like the narcissist is that normal people usually like to fix broken things. Narcissists are broken people, and hence, a normal person wants to fix him so that he changes.

Trauma bonding occurs from trauma to your emotions over and over again, and it occurs through passive aggressive manipulation that a narcissist is a master at.

This brings us to the question of what causes trauma bonding.

The condition leading to trauma bonding emphasizes two controlling types of reinforcement that occur one after the other at perfectly scheduled intervals. This reinforcement is called as the "*arousal jag.*" The term refers to the exhilaration before the trauma (arousal) and the harmony that comes from the submission (jag).

Arousal-jag reinforcement is all about giving a little and then taking it away over and over in periodic intervals. Narcissists do this all the time (by showering praises and then insulting, by appearing and then disappearing) and create a delusion of some sort of twisted exhilaration that emphasizes the traumatic bond between the two parties involved.

Why Does the Narcissist Do This?

The narcissist does this because he derives excitement knowing what is going to come in the future. The narcissist is aware of the control he is going to be able to exert on you and how dependent you will become on him. Therefore, narcissists always have more than one partner, as it increases their excitement factor. The fact that you become so attached to the chaos that you eagerly wait for him and are ready to fulfill all his demands and tolerate abuse is the cherry on the cake.

Hope you can make sense with this information about the crazy behavior of the narcissist. Yes, you read that right. It is the narcissist who with his crazy ways is driving you crazy so that he can use that at a later stage to tell the entire world how crazy and mad you are. That is his functioning style.

The devalue stage is when the trauma is carried out by the narcissist. In this stage, he subjects you to betrayal and neglect. The key point here is that even before the narcissist has begun the trauma, your body indicates to you that there is something terrible that is going to happen by showing symptoms such as a "knot in the stomach" feeling that refuses to go.

The sad truth is by now you have become addicted to their behavior and everything that goes with it. You become dependent on them and wait for the moment with desperation. You start longing for him/her until you can barely tolerate it anymore. Then suddenly the narcissist appears to give you the second reinforcement: the peace of surrender that happens afterward. Their return is perfectly scheduled to have a perfect impact, which is followed by a silent treatment. The narcissist is conditioning you to accept less and less so they can get away with more each time they vanish or torture you. This is his how they exert control.

The second dose of reinforcement where you actually surrender to the narcissist is when you have gotten your dose and you are at peace. You love surrendering to all the drama that they created because surrendering makes your anxiety vanish, and after what feels like ages, you sense peace within you. This cycle repeats at regular intervals as and when the narcissist decides. They decide when to appear and then disappears, keeping you waiting. Throughout this process, unknowingly you being to enjoy this cycle, and you are extremely happy when it happens.

Under normal circumstances, you would try to escape from such an abusive person, especially when you are the subject of all the abuse. But with a narcissist, nothing is normal, because he has set the stage for abnormality to continue. The cycles of reinforcing positivity followed by negativity create an unhealthy dynamic from which you cannot escape. Through the course of this book, I refer to the narcissist as a he, but please understand that females are narcissist too, and they are equally as toxic, malicious and perpetrate as much evil to their victims as the male counterparts. My heart goes out to male survivors for many reasons. Firstly, it must be very difficult for them to even admit that they are being abused, because society expects men to always be strong and in charge, and the stereotype is that men are the narcissist and psychopaths, making it easy for their abusers to get away with smear campaigns. There are many organizations and shelters for female survivors that offer support but I've not heard of a shelter for men yet. Most of the support groups for victims of psychological abuse are dominated by women too. However, male survivors should understand more the nature of psychological abuse, it has absolutely noting to do with how macho they are physically. Female narcissist operates in a different way from males, most of them are sneaky and use more manipulative tactics to gain control over their victims. There are some that are very physically aggressive too. So while I use he or him to describe the narcissist some times, its just because my experience was with a man, and everyone in my group is female too. However the principles strategies I would discuss, can be applied for Male survivors as well.

The Stages of Narcissistic Trauma Bonding

A narcissist works on creating a stage where he keeps inflicting you with humiliation, followed by praise in stages. He decides how long each stage lasts and when to proceed to the next stage.

The first stage is when the narcissist is trying to set up the trap for you to fall. In this stage, he praises you for everything that you, showers you with gifts, and is so charming, trying to woo you.

By the time the second stage arrives, you are completely dependent on the narcissist and need their presence in your life. You believe that they are your soul mate, and the narcissist understands that you have been trapped.

The third stage is when the narcissist abuses for the first time. This is the when they slowly start the abuse and test the waters to see how much you can tolerate and how far you will go to appease them.

They do this by controlling you and humiliating you, and you begin to doubt yourself.

By the fourth stage, you begin doubting yourself and believe their facts as the narcissist resorts to a technique called as "gaslighting," in which they make you believe that you are at fault by constantly blaming you, and changing facts.

By the last stage, firm control has been established over you by the narcissist. You have lost your sense of self and identity and no longer envision a life without the narcissist. Your near and dear ones can spot something amiss in you, but you cannot spot the changes in you. By this stage, you are just like a drug addict who is addicted to the narcissist. You start craving their presence and will do nothing to upset the equation.

Intermittent Reinforcement

Many researchers have focused on making healthy lab rats to press a bar, hoping that they would get a continuous supply of food. The researchers' goal was to keep the rats working for rewards even after they had stopped giving them any. Lab rats were chosen because rats are known to react like human beings in most situations.

It was found out that by intermittently reinforcing rewards and then snatching the reward, which can be equated to punishment or the discard phase, the rats were very eager and waiting for the reinforcement to happen.

If you apply this to your situation, you may recall that every time the narcissist vanishes or punishes you, you start longing for him, and the longing becomes unbearable after a certain point. It is exactly like how a drug addict feels when the supply gets over. You become desperate for the attention and long for "arousal" phase.

You must be wondering how the narcissist understands or knows this?

The narcissist is extremely intelligent and has a complete understanding of the functioning of the brain without any training or education. They are pro at reading people and choose their targets after a lot of observation. If you recall, the initial stages of the relationship are where the narcissist is observing you or rather judging you to see whether you fit the bill.

How Did You Fit the Bill?

The narcissists usually target Empaths. These are

people who have a high degree of empathy and always put others' needs over their needs. This is what the narcissist wants. He wants a person who will submit to his whims and fancies and completely surrender.

Only an empath can do that because it is the natural personality of an empath to put the needs of other's first.

You fit the bill because the narcissist has identified that you are an empath, and hence, you can easily be manipulated and made to surrender. A narcissist will rarely waste his time if he does not think you fit the bill.

So the trauma bond is formed, and the narcissist works on strengthening this trauma bond so much that it becomes impossible for you to break it because the key to it is with the narcissist.

The longer the relationship goes on, the more difficult it is to break this bond. Therefore, you see so many intelligent, capable, and professionally successful women unable to break off from the narcissist's clutches.

Things become more difficult when children are involved. This is because for centuries women have been conditioned to think that their fundamental duty is to raise a family and protect the family at all costs. Women have been told that they must forgive their husbands and change the man.

Apart from social conditioning, women also find it hard to leave because as discussed above the narcissist will ensure that you are depleted of all support. He will isolate you from friends and family, take away your finances, and mess up your life by damaging your self-confidence and soul.

With nowhere to go and a damaged spirit, people like you suffer silently and bear the torture.

Confusion

It is common for victims to feel confused all the time because the narcissist makes you doubt yourself. The narcissist achieves this by constantly crossing your boundaries and constantly shouting at you and blaming you for everything, and soon you begin to lose a sense of what you did, and what you did not and the confusion begins. It is extremely confusing for you because you are being held responsible for his abusive behavior, and this soon becomes a pattern. This is compounded by the fact that every time you begin to question the torture you are subjected to, the narcissist deflects the blame back to you by convincing you that you were wrong. Hence, you feel confused all the time. The narcissist used you, that's what they do really well, use people.

Suicidal Thoughts

The sad truth about experiencing narcissistic abuse is that you start developing suicidal feelings. You must be wondering why you are experiencing suicidal thoughts?

This is because the narcissist works at destroying your core by oscillating between periods of good and bad behavior. During the bad behavior phase, he credits you to all his outburst and blames you for everything. This constant change between periods of good and bad confuses you. During the bad phase, he humiliates you by calling you names, gaslighting you, and eventually making you lose trust in yourself. The narcissist causes shame and instills fear in you leaving you crippled and lost.

They get away with it partly because you ignore the abuse and try to rationalize all the bad behavior and slowly start accepting their blame. Over some time, your self-esteem takes a beating, and you are left with no self-respect and confidence.

No matter how strong you are as a person, there is a limit to how much torture you can accept, and finally, you begin to crumble. This is why suicidal thoughts develop, coupled with depression and loneliness.

Feeling Crazy

A lot of times you may feel like you are the crazy one and that the narcissist is true in calling you crazy. This happens because, during your relationship, you would have been a silent spectator to their constant denial of things, which they said or did. They have the innate ability to deny things immediately and turn the tables around by questioning or worse interrogating you. This makes you doubt yourself, and you get confused thereby thinking that you are crazy. In addition to denial, they also conveniently blame you for things that did not go according to their way or due to their fault. A narcissist will never agree that he is wrong and will torture you till you accept. Soon you start accepting everything they have said to calm down the narcissist.

This technique of denying or altering the truth to suit their needs is called gaslighting. It is a powerful technique used by abusers such as the narcissist to make the victim doubt themselves, and eventually, the victims begin to question their own sanity.

Another reason you feel crazy is that whenever you summon the courage and try to argue with a narcissist by pointing out his mistake, they are quick to negate it. Arguments with a narcissist are bound to make you feel crazy because they are a never-ending cycle of nonsense and blame deflection. Ultimately, you will end up losing the argument because the narcissist will drain your energy and you give up.

Effect on the Brain

By now you know that exposure to narcissistic abuse causes PTSD, which causes flashbacks and nightmares.

But did you know that exposure to narcissistic abuse also has major effects on the brain? Yes, that is right. Apart from taking an emotional toll on a person and affecting the body physically by causing muscle aches and body pain, abuse also affects the brain.

It affects two aspects of the brain—the hippocampus and the amygdala. The hippocampus is crucial for learning and development of memories, while the amygdala is responsible for negative emotions such as shame, guilt, fear, and envy.

With constant exposure to abuse, it has been observed that the hippocampus shrinks in size and the amygdala swells in size. This is dangerous because both of these lead to long-term damage and devastating effects.

Have You Wondered Why Memory Loss Occurs during Abuse?

Well, that is because the hippocampus is the element associated with memory in the human brain. It is specifically responsible for short-term memory. All memories are first stored as short-term memory before they can be converted to long-term memory. Damage to the hippocampus is dangerous because this implies no learning, as there is no short-term memory.

It has been observed that people with high levels of stress have smaller hippocampus as compared to ordinary people.

The amygdala controls the emotions such as lust, anger, and fear, shame, etc., as well heart rate and breathing. The flight-or-fight response that you experience as a result of abuse is triggered here in the amygdala. The amygdala is constantly on alert when you are experiencing narcissistic abuse because the narcissist is doing everything possible that is causing stress to you. Eventually, you will end up falling into a constant state of anxiety and fear, and thus, the amygdala is enlarged or swollen. This is the way the amygdala responds to abuse and stress caused by the abuse.

This is why even though your relationship with the narcissist has ended, you continue to have symptoms of PTSD, nightmares, and flashbacks because your amygdala is used to being in that state.

When the hippocampus is damaged or stressed, it releases a hormone called cortisol. The cortisol attacks the neurons in the hippocampus, thus reducing the size. The cortisol also activates the amygdala, which gets stimulated.

After reading all this, you may be worried that can you ever become normal again and lead a healthy normal life.

The good news is *yes*. *Yes*, you can break free and lead a completely normal life. This will require time and patience but is not unachievable.

In the next chapters, you will be taught how to heal and regain your life back from the clutches of the narcissist.

How Do You Reverse the Damage Done to the Hippocampus and Amygdala?

As you know, the brain is one of the most important organs in your body, and hence, the first thing you need to understand is how the damage done to the hippocampus and amygdala can be reversed so that you can live a normal, healthy, and stress-free life.

There are several scientific methods available to help you reverse the damage done. Some of them are eye movement desensitization and reprocessing theory, or EMDR, which has shown to help victims with PTSD. EMDR has shown to help improve both the hippocampus and amygdala and hence can be extremely beneficial in your healing journey.

There are also therapy sessions available where you can seek the help of professionals and therapists trained to treat victims of narcissistic abuse.

A lot of spiritual techniques such as meditation, using essential oils in aromatherapy, and acts of altruism have shown positive results in victims of narcissistic abuse. Apart from these, another technique called emotional freedom technique has shown to be useful in normalizing the biochemical short-circuiting, which is present in cases of extreme anxiety. Emotional freedom technique is a form of professional intervention that uses alternative medicine concepts such as acupuncture, neuro-linguistic programming and energy medicine.

What Do You Think About This Book so Far?

I hope this book has met your expectations so far. Please take a minute to leave feedback
CLICK HERE

Any suggestion on how the information does or does not meet your expectations are welcome. A kind review would mean more than you know.

Thank you.

Emma

Chapter Three: Healing from Narcissistic Abuse

You might have noticed that in your previous breakups, you would have moved after grieving for a while.

All breakups are disastrous because you pictured a happy ending, but sadly, that did not happen, but you deal with it and move on, but dealing with a breakup with a narcissist is like conquering the Mount Everest, which is the tallest peak in the world.

This is because, as discussed in the previous chapters, the narcissist damages you from within. This requires a healing touch, as it is similar to recovering after a deadly disease.

It can be extremely demotivating to you because every time you take a step forward, you realize you are being pulled backward by two steps immediately. This back-and-forth keeps happening until one fine day when you do not move backward anymore.

One of the most difficult things while healing from

narcissistic abuse is the shifting dynamic between extreme anger you feel for what happened and immediately shifting to ruminating about the good times that gain momentum to drag you into dreaming of a happy union.

The mind knows what happened was wrong and hence the anger, but the heart still keeps thinking only about the good phases.

These conflicting emotions between your own heart and mind are what make healing a tedious task.

This cognitive dissonance is the root cause of all the delay in healing, and the most important step is to rid yourself the confusion.

Which means that once your mind and heart start communicating and speak the same language, that is when true healing happens, and you become completely free.

Upon finally accepting all that has happened, you might be shocked, unable to comprehend how a seemingly normal person could torture another person so much. You must understand that narcissists are not normal people like you and I. They have always been like this, and this is their "normal" way of functioning.

All your good traits of compassion, forgiveness, and empathy run so deep within you that all this while you were trying to make sense of the narcissist's behavior and giving him the benefit of the doubt. You are taught about the virtues of forgiveness and showing empathy and compassion to troubled souls, and that is exactly what you did.

Hence, you *must* not blame yourself because you did everything right. God has finally led you to the path of awakening, and it is your faith and goodness that has brought you to this juncture where you can start the process of healing.

Healing from abuse and learning to walk away is like learning to walk all over again. Look around and observe how toddlers learn to walk. They do not start walking and running immediately, do they? It is a slow process, which involves falling several times, yet the toddler persists and finally can walk.

Your healing journey is similar to that. Consider yourself a child; when you fall, remember, it is temporary, get up, and start again. All this can be exhausting, but remember, nothing worth it comes easy in life, and there are no free lunches either. You have to earn every bit of it.

If you are truly ready to heal, there are a few key

points you must consider.

- You must be ready to do through self-introspection—learn about yourself, your childhood.

- You must learn to set boundaries and implement them.

- You must learn what issues you have that allowed you to stay with a narcissist. This is because the narcissist was able to do whatever he did because he saw some issues within you. This is not like blaming yourself, but rather self-exploration to identify the concerns within you. Identifying these will help you tackle them so that you do not let this happen again in future.

- Last but not least, *stop* expecting the narcissist to take accountability and accept whatever he did. A narcissist will *never* accept he is wrong, and if he does accept, it is all false promises, and he will never keep up.

This is *your* journey of healing, and it is best to keep the narcissist out of this for your own good.

You must understand that this is going to be a long process with several stages to your recovery process.

Stages of recovery from narcissistic abuse can be classified into the following:

Denial

This is the first phase in which you will most likely find yourself. In this stage, you conclude that the relationship is over, but you are unable to process it. Against your own better judgment, you cannot help but fantasize about a happy reunion. You run through multiple scenarios of what-ifs, trying to see if you can make things work. So many survivors find it to much to handle as they succumb to the emotional turmoil and return back to the relationship at this stage, however they soon realize that the abuser is never going to change, and the circle of abuse gets even worse. There would be no healing if a victim chooses the fantasy of a perfect loving partner and continues to chase after that instead of choosing to love and protect themselves.

Anger

This is the stage when anger is the dominant emotion. All you will feel is anger—anger at yourself that you let this happen to you, anger at the abuser for causing all the trauma, anger at the world for not understanding you or trusting you, and finally anger at God. This is the stage when a lot of people start disbelieving in the supreme power and turn bitter. You might catch yourself blaming God for all this and not protecting you and guiding you on the right path.

You do this because you need to blame someone. It is a human tendency to try to find something or someone who can be blamed for the situation, and this does not make you a bad person or a bad Christian, but it is also important to remember that anger needs to be channelized in the right manner and not negatively. Your job is to turn this negative emotion of anger into your strength. This is when you must join a nearby gym class or kickboxing classes or take the help of a therapist. Exercise will help you get out all your anger and make you strong.

This is also the phase where because of the anger and rage boiling within you, you want to send angry hate mails to your abuser. Refrain from doing so as this will only help the narcissist understand that you are still thinking about him, and remember all that a narcissist wants is attention, so while you are writing hate mails, the narcissist will be rejoicing thinking that he still has the power to disturb you. Hence, channelize your anger in the right manner.

Bargaining

In this stage, you start bargaining, which is trying to find out ways and means to make this relationship work and give it the happy ending of your dreams. Bargaining and denial go hand in hand, and you could be experiencing both at the same time. It is during this phase that you may think that you have all the power to negotiate and change the narcissist. After all, you have been told that people change and you can change a person. You take this belief seriously and start thinking of ways and means to negotiate with the narcissist to bring about a change. This is also the phase when you may take the help of friends and family to talk to the narcissist.

Depression

Just like anger, depression has many myriad forms. It comes in all shapes and sizes and attacks you. In this face, you are down with hopelessness because you slowly begin to understand the true impact of what has happened to you, and you are left with no choice but to face it. The book Healing from hidden abuse by Shannon Thomas is a great resource for learning how to tackle all the challenges that come at all the different stages of healing from psychological abuse. If you notice signs of depression, please seek for professional help, and if you cannot afford therapy reach out to family and friends and talk to someone. Tell them exactly how you feel and don't be afraid to be direct by saying things as they are. Saying 'I have been feeling down lately' is not the same as 'I have been considering taking my own life'. Depression is a disease and you must try to fight it accordingly.

Acceptance

Congratulations to you for reaching the final stage of recovery and healing. In this stage, you finally accept whatever has happened and make peace with it. It happens very gradually and over some time, and finally, you will get up one fine morning without any depression or soreness. You will suddenly feel light and start feeling positive emotions such as joy, happiness, and above all, peace of mind.

This is the ultimate goal of the recovery process. Once you have reached acceptance, you will realize that the thoughts about the narcissist will not cause a breakdown in you and send you crying buckets. You will realize that suddenly you do not experience panic attacks, flashbacks, or nightmares anymore, and after what feels like centuries, you can sleep peacefully at night. The narcissist does not have any power or control over you, and you are truly *free*.

It is important to know the various phases of recovery because this will help you understand yourself and be patient with yourself. It will help you normalize the entire process and give you the necessary strength.

You may be wondering if the day will ever come when you will reach the acceptance stage.

It is normal to think this way, especially when it looks like there is no progress being made, but there is light at the end of the tunnel, after all. At the end of this long and daunting journey, you *will* emerge victoriously and as a better, confident, and assertive person.

There will be times when it will seem like you have progressed to a new stage only to realize the next morning that you have gone back to stage one. The recovery process does not exactly happen in the order in which the steps have been mentioned, though complete acceptance is the last stage. There will be times when you will be going through two or more stages at the same time.

Throughout the stages of recovery, you may experience extreme trust issues and not be able to trust anyone. You can also become paranoid that everyone you meet is a narcissist and has an ulterior motive.

How to Heal from the Narcissistic Abuse

Finally, here you are at the most important topic that is going to change your life for good and forever. After reading the previous chapters, you now know and understand that *you* are, after all, not all crazy and that what happened to you was never your fault.

After going through the stages of grief and finally reaching acceptance, it is now important to understand how to heal from the abuse and lead a healthy life full of joy and happiness.

There are two fundamental concepts that you need to keep in mind and implement every single day of your life if you want to heal completely.

- Setting firm boundaries
- No contact or gray rock

Setting firm boundaries. Once you have accepted the abuse that was meted out to you, it is now time for the healing process to begin. Healing of the wounds caused to your mind and soul that cannot be seen by the outside world but can only be felt by you. For the healing to commence, it is important that you build and set firm boundaries.

What Does Building and Setting Boundaries Mean?

Have you ever wondered why homes have fences or apartments have gates? Why does your home have a door? Why don't you leave the door to your home open?

The answer is simple and obvious. It is because you do not want to allow enemies or strangers to enter your premises. It is because you want to protect your space and your privacy.

This is exactly why you need boundaries while healing from the narcissistic abuse as well. If you think about it, the reason the narcissist was able to enter your mind and body and wreak havoc is that you did not enforce boundaries. You let him in with open arms, and he caused the damage.

It is not wrong to love openly, but it is harmful to love without boundaries because without boundaries, there is no protection, so you need to set firm boundaries and communicate the same to the narcissist.

Remember, a narcissist does not care about you or the boundaries that you set. He will do everything in his power to break them and exert control over you because the narcissist's main goal is his happiness at the cost of your destruction.

Even after you have communicated the boundaries, the narcissist will not stop contacting you. He will beg, plead or threaten you to let you into his life. It is here that implementing boundaries comes into the picture. *Do not budge* and break the boundaries you established and allow them back into your life. Remember, if you do that, you let go of the control you have on your life, as the narcissist will take back the control, in no time.

A narcissist will contact you to test waters and see your reaction. Do not show your emotions to him. You might be seething with rage inside, but on the surface, you must act normal and unaffected because the narcissist cannot tolerate being ignored.

Another way to reinforce boundaries is by learning to say a firm *no*. It is important for you to understand that *no* is a complete sentence by itself and does not need further explanations. Learning to say *no* will help you build self-respect and confidence apart from establishing boundaries that will protect you. This is the boundary you are building to protect your mind and body. It will keep positivity in and negativity out.

It is very important to establish and enforce boundaries because they give you a sense of identity as they define what you want and what you do not want. A narcissist main aim is to damage your identity, and hence, boundaries need to be enforced if you want to reclaim and protect your identity.

Your mind automatically senses danger when your boundaries are being compromised. This is because the body and mind are built in that manner. Remember, all the times when you felt uncomfortable with the narcissist when he was doing something or expecting something from you and your boundaries were being compromised. The uneasy sensation in your body is its way of telling you things are wrong. During the relationship with the narcissist, you learn to silence this voice to keep the relationship intact.

Make a list of all that is important to you. This can be anything from what makes you angry, what hurts you, and what is against your interest or belief system. Keep reminding yourself these, and every time you feel a sense of uneasiness, immediately check which of your boundaries are being compromised. You need to train your brain to work in this manner.

By honoring your boundaries, you will be honoring yourself and thus building your self-respect back. Be explicit about communicating your boundaries, and do not expect anyone to read your mind or the situation and understand. Say what you feel and believe and stick to it.

No Contact

This is often the hardest part of the entire journey, but this is also the second most important part of the healing journey after setting boundaries.

How do you implement no contact?

No contact can be implemented by completely cutting off contact from all possible means of communication. This means blocking the narcissist from all social media accounts and blocking them on the phone as well.

No contact is the way to remove the toxic person out from your life so that you can live a happier, healthier life while trying to rebuild yourself. No contact is the way in which a person is truly blocked from your heart, mind, and spirit.

It is important to establish no contact because this is the only way to deal with from the complex trauma bonds that are established when in a relationship with a narcissist. If you remain in constant contact with the abuser, then you are not giving yourself the necessary time to heal and get better.

No contact will give you time away from the trauma by helping you focus on *you*, something that you can never do with the narcissist around because they want all the attention.

No contact will help you grieve in peace and focus on yourself and heal from the ending of the unhealthy relationship. It is also established so that the narcissist understands that you have finally seen through his personality, and this will prevent them from coming back into your life.

Full no contact means blocking both in person and virtual world. This means restricting access and not leaving behind any way by which the narcissist can contact or reach you. You must also block the person from calling you and messaging you, even sending emails. This is because the narcissist will try all means to get back to you not because he loves you or misses you but because he misses having a target in his life. You must also avoid the temptation to find out about him through the third party or common friends and family members. It helps to remove triggers such as photographs, gifts, and anything else that might remind you of him.

Always refuse all requests to meet up even for a few minutes because all it takes is a few minutes for the narcissist to manipulate you. It may also mean that you cut contact with any friends you have made through him because he will use them to manipulate you. There are also cases where a narcissist would discard their victim, and block them on all social platforms with no explanation. This can be exceptionally though, especially when the relationship has been going on for years. Now the victim feels that the narcissist owes them an explanation. They feel hurt because no one wants to feel like they don't matter, no one wants to be discarded like trash.

I met Sandra in church, and I was immediately drawn to her because she always looked put together and fashionable. We got close over time and she shared with me how she was able to recover from heartbreak and abuse. In her situation, she wasn't married to the narcissist, but they had been together for about seven years. He had a previous relationship where he had kids. He would shower her with gifts and money, and she liked nice things so she stayed, even though she knew he was having affairs with multiple women. He promised to marry her several times, and on one occasion, they printed out cards, she shopped for a wedding dress, they went as far as paying vendors only for him to cancel just a few days before the wedding. Still she stayed with him. Over the years, she had made her believe that no one else wanted her, and the only thing she was good for was sex. The day he discarded her finally, he moved back in with the mother of his kids, who he apparently had still been with all along. The sad part was she knew nothing about Narcissist until years after. The confusion, betrayal and pain she shared with me, broke my heart.

The Breaking of No Contact

As stated above, this is the most difficult part of the healing journey, and at times you will find yourself desperate to reply to his messages or frequent the places he visits to catch a glimpse of him.

This happens because strong trauma bonds have been established and these bonds make you crave the abuser. For you to heal completely and regain your life, it is essential that you break the trauma bonds. It is inevitable that you may relapse, but remember that every time you fall, you will rise again. If it becomes very difficult to maintain no contact, then immerse yourself in distraction such as taking classes or attending meditation sessions. Do not resist the urge to grieve. Grieving is a natural

process, and curbing it will not make
vanish.

During the process of no contact, ther
ments when you will face unbearable grief and longing to go back. It is during such times that you must show resilience and have the strength to resist the urge to go back. When you face such a situation, let the emotions pour. Do not resist the negative emotions because they will go nowhere. The more you suppress them, the more you are pushing them into your system and the more havoc they will create.

Instead, learn how to accept the emotions and deal with them. Initially, you may have breakdowns and cry for hours together, but slowly you will realize that with time the intensity of the breakdowns will reduce, and ultimately, you will not break down.

You can curb the craving for breaking no contact by practicing mindfulness. Mindfulness is the wonderful concept which talks about being present in the moment. Remember that this too shall pass and that it is temporary. You will eventually realize that no contact has huge benefits, and it will not be long before you see the fruits of your labor.

No contact is the wonderful opportunity you are

.ving yourself. It can feel strange because your past must have been spent trying to keep up with the narcissist's tantrums and rage. You have forgotten what it means to spend time with yourself and take care of yourself. This is why everything feels strange initially. Now that you are finally giving yourself a chance, your mind and body will take some time to get used to it. Consider this to be a detox to your body and mind, where you are flushing out all the toxic memories of a person whose only aim was to harm you.

The best way to keep yourself motivated is to keep a journal where you can track your progress. Write down briefly every little progress you have made, and you will be amazed at how far you have come in the journey.

When you avoid no contact there, you are setting yourself up for a path of defeat. Some other self-defeating accomplishments as a result of avoiding no contact are as follows:

- You take away credibility for your boundaries that you set thereby indicating to the abuser that you do not care for yourself.
- You will also show the narcissist that you are ready to accept them back and give them

another chance which they do not deserve.

- You will set yourself up for a no strings attached relationship with no accountability.
- You will be making yourself into a fallback option for the narcissist, conveying to them that they can always rely on you for supply.
- You will start to loathe yourself every time you realize how you went back to them. Self-loathing will never lead you to recovery.

A narcissist has great confidence that they can win you back because they will never doubt their abilities to con you once again. It is in your hands to avoid this situation. Hence, do not break the "no contact" rule at any cost if you want to heal and move ahead completely. Remember too that if you do, you need to forgive yourself quickly and start over again. It is very common for most victims to break no contact, do not be hard on yourself. Healing is a process and with determination you will reach your goals. Always be kind to yourself. No contact can be tough, and you have to take intentional measures to ensure that you succeed. A few things that worked for me and the woman in our little group, are prayer and studying the word of God, Journaling, and keeping one another accountable. I cannot over emphasize the power of finding a safe group of people to support you in this journey. Though there is just four of us in our little group, we talk often and have been a great source of inspiration to one another. I am also a member of a few Facebook support groups of narcissistic abuse survivors, and those too have been very beneficial.

How to Implement No Contact When Children Are Involved?

When it comes to establishing no contact, by now, you would have understood that it is extremely important to maintain no contact because of the trauma bonds that develop.

Things become further complicated with a child or children involved. It is a very well-established fact that parenting children is a herculean task even without family issues involved. Parenting or rather co-parenting with a narcissist is an altogether different mountain that you need to scale. This needs to be handled differently so that the child and you do not get damaged further.

In cases where children are involved absolute, “no contact” cannot be implemented, and the narcissist will use this to his advantage. The narcissist understands that you cannot establish a “no contact” rule because you cannot prevent them from visiting their children. Because it is not possible to block them, move away, refuse to take their calls, or refuse to open the door for them when they show up at your home when children are involved.

By now you are aware that a narcissist is not psychologically normal and hence, they will never be a normal parent. A narcissist will use the children by manipulating them to fulfill their selfish needs. They would try to instigate the child against you and will assassinate your character in front of the child. All this can be very daunting and damaging, but through this all, you must never lose faith and trust. Have faith in yourself and God that one day your children will see the truth. You cannot control what the narcissist will tell the children, but you can control your message to the children. This happens because the narcissist's mask will slip away, and he will eventually expose himself. It is important for you not to follow this route, to say negative things about your ex to the children because that would be more abusive to them. Instead, maintain a positive outlook on everything, and if you don't have anything nice to say, then say nothing at all. If your kids are old enough, you can educate them about Narcissism, and they can be better equipped to protect themselves from abuse too.

Parental Alienation

Parental alienation means when one parent tries to turn the children against the other parent. This is very commonly seen in the case of a narcissist. A narcissist is very angry with you for implementing no contact and trying to regain your life. This happens because he understands that he no longer has the power or control over you, which he previously had, and this is something that the narcissist cannot tolerate. This loss of control coupled with the loss of attention becomes a dangerous concoction that the narcissist cannot ingest, and hence, he will do anything to damage you.

This is where parental alienation comes into the picture. Though a narcissist may not know the term parental alienation, he knows for sure that by turning the children against and creating hatred in the children for you, you will be damaged, and he can win again.

A narcissist does this by blaming you in front of the children for the collapse of the relationship, falsely accusing you of everything, and even resorting to character assassination. He may try to manipulate the children and distort your image in their heads. For the narcissist parent, children are just another target to be used for fulfilling their desire. The narcissist will treat children as pawns in his battle against you.

A narcissist does all this because in his head, he is the victim and you are wrong. Strange as it may sound to you, but a narcissist thoroughly believes that he lost his rights, and thus, he now wants to engage in a battle with you and destroy you. He feels humiliated and like a victim because you have stopped giving him attention and have taken back the control. He may also recruit other family members and friends to fight with him against you because he has managed to con them just like he did with you in the past.

If you sense any abuse during the narcissist's interaction with the children or if you sense a behavioral change in the child, then you should document what you observe and contact the Child Protective Services. If the child refuses to go along with the narcissistic parent or refuses interaction with such a parent and instead complains to you, then you have to believe the child and give him the attention he needs. In a lot of states in the US, children, especially over the age of twelve, have the right to refuse interacting or visiting the narcissist parent and cannot be forced to comply. If your children are very young and you are convinced that regular interactions with the narcissist are going to harm them and disturb their mental state, then you can work with your attorney to limit interactions or stop them if the need arises.

This is especially true in cases where the children have expressed their displeasure and have clearly stated they do not want to meet the narcissist. Honor their request, and do not force them. You can ask your children to narrate whatever happened and listen patiently without being judgmental. Make notes about it as this can be useful in court battles.

You need to put in the extra effort to minimize damage and ensure that your progress is not stalled. Begin by understanding that there is no concept of co-parenting with a narcissist.

What you must instead do instead of “no contact” is to learn and practice the art of “no reaction.” No reaction means that you do not show any emotion, be it positive or negative, such as the anger you hold for him, in front of the narcissist. When you come face-to-face with a narcissist or when you are engaging with him over other means of communication such as phone calls, text messages, or email, limit the conversation to the topic concerned, which should be ideally only related to the children. Do not respond or show any reaction to any other topic the narcissist brings up in his attempts to rekindle the relationship. This is due to the fact a narcissist thrives on your reaction. Any reaction is better for him than no reaction because a no reaction means you are ignoring him, and a narcissist cannot handle being ignored.

Dealing with a narcissist is like playing a game of tug of war with a rope. The game goes till both sides are pulling with all their might, but the moment one person drops the rope; there is no game to be played. Similarly, with the narcissist, the minute you stop reacting, the game stops, and the narcissist knows that now he does not have control over you.

Like any other skill in life, no reaction is a skill that needs to be cultivated consciously. You need to practice it every day because even a minute of negligence can bring the narcissist back. You have every right to protect yourself and your sanity. Hence, develop strict boundaries and implement them along with no reaction. Initially, it is going to be very difficult. You may have a seething rage to reply to that email or to shout at them, or you may even believe the false claims of being a changed person. *Never* let them know what you are thinking. You can always let out your emotions when you are alone or confide with someone whom you can trust.

How to Co-Parent with a Narcissist

Establish firm boundaries around the home and school. Develop strong boundaries related to your children and communicate the same to the narcissist. Ensure that the communication is firm, and implement it on a regular basis. This kind of discipline and structure can also provide a safe environment to children and reduce the psychological damage a child undergoes.

If a narcissist shows up uninvited or when a meeting with the children has not been fixed, then you *should not* open the door and entertain him. You always have to communicate in a firm voice about how he can fix a meeting on the phone and come back at the designated time.

Maintain Documentation

When co-parenting with a narcissist, it is important to maintain thorough documentation of everything. Maintain a journal and write down every incident by date and time, as much as you can. Speak with your child after every interaction with the narcissist and try to gather as much information as possible. It is better to write everything as and when it happens so that you do not forget anything. Things to be included can be the time he comes to pick up children if he is late or early for the meeting, parent-teacher meetings at school and what is spoken, and the kids' behavior before and after the meeting with the narcissist.

If you sense any change in the behavior of the children, then make detailed notes and gather any evidence as well. This information can be used when you report the matter to Child Services. Ensure that all communication is done through email or texting so that there is a written record of what he said as it is. This is due to the fact that if the conversations only happen on the phone, then the narcissist can turn tables and completely deny the conversations. Hence, even if something is discussed over the phone, always ask for a written confirmation of the same.

Good documentation will make court battles easy since the narcissist cannot deny. If he denies anything, then you can produce the written proof that you have gathered. I understand that this can be a lot to handle alongside caring for kids and a busy schedule, but it is important because you have found yourself in very peculiar circumstances, and you must protect yourself and your children.

Do Not Criticize the Narcissist in Front of the Children

It can be tempting to bash the narcissist in front of children, but refrain from doing so. This is because if the children are young, then they do not have the emotional maturity yet to process it, and also the narcissist may get back to you saying that you are influencing the children. This can become an issue as the narcissist is always looking out for an opportunity to get back at you.

This can also stop people from trusting your claims, because to the outside world, the narcissists are model citizens who go to church every Sunday, pay their bills and taxes on time, and are very good at work. Hence, it is best to hold back your anger and not criticize him.

Triangulation

Triangulation means bringing another person or a group of people into the relationship to demean the victim and make the victim desperate for the abuser. A narcissist is an expert at triangulation and will use this tactic especially when children are involved.

He can do this by putting the kids in a spot or by bringing in someone else to talk badly about you to the kids so that the kids start believing him. Become aware of triangulation and document it. If you think that it is becoming dangerous then reach out for help.

Educate Your Kids

You are the best judge of the situation, and hence as and when deemed appropriate by you, educate your kids about the situation and provide them with safety tips. This education will help them to protect themselves when they find themselves alone with the narcissist. Empower your kids and encourage them to be honest with you and always inculcate trust.

Seek a Parent Coordinator through the Court

The court can decide to appoint a parent coordinator in case of high-conflict cases. Once a parent coordinator has been appointed, all scheduling activities and communication can be through the coordinator, thus avoiding the pain to you. Parent coordinators are trained personnel usually and come with experience in handling such cases. You can speak with your attorney and see if you need one and can avail the services.

Have a Guardian for the Children

In case you are fighting for custody, then you can have a guardian ad litem (GAL) appointed for the children. The guardian will look after the best interests of the children while you are fighting in the court. The guardian can provide children with the necessary support and act as an advocate and support person. Consult your attorney to see if this can be arranged.

Refuse to Make Your Child a Pawn

It can be very tempting to use your child as a pawn and send children out on a fact-finding mission when they are with the narcissistic parent. Refrain from doing this, as the children will very quickly understand that they are being used, and this will damage them. Do not interrogate your kids about things that are happening in the narcissist's house. If the children want to talk, then you can listen. You must also identify if the narcissist is trying to communicate to you through the children by using them as messengers and sending gifts or communication through them. Do not accept the gifts, and send a firm message back to him that this will not be entertained, and school him on how he cannot be using the children as pawns.

Have a Detailed Custody Agreement

Consult your attorney and get them to draft a detailed custody agreement with even the smallest details laid down. You must have every detail mentioned such as what percentage of medical costs will be paid by the narcissist, clear mention of visitation times, and period of visit each time with other specifications about visitations during holiday times.

Child Counseling

If needed, you can take the help of child counselors. This may be needed because, during high-conflict battles such as the one with the narcissist, children can get affected deeply and may not even be able to articulate their feelings. They may internalize everything that can lead to deep scarring and damage them for life. Child counselors can help your children deal with the trauma of the separation, as well as help them handle conversations with the narcissist in the future. You can get this included in the custody agreement by speaking with your attorney.

Manage Your Expectations

You must remember that narcissists don't change. The turmoil and commotion they create isn't about you. Just like while you were in a relationship, they made you feel like you were never good enough, through co-parenting also, they are going to make you feel the same way. This happens because putting the other person off balance is what a narcissist does best, and they will continue doing that always. Don't wait for them to change, take the onus on you, don't be empathetic or give in to their desire for control over you and the children. Learn to manage your expectations to save your sanity and progress in life. Knowing that they won't change and expecting nothing back will help you plan out your next strategy and calmly deal with the situation. This will also help you practice no reaction and implementing boundaries in a better manner.

Still in Love with the Abuser?

You have successfully managed to read this book so far, and you must have had made "aha" moments.

You now can give a name to your feelings, understand PTSD, and also know about trauma bonding and the devastating effect it can have on your mind and body.

But deep inside you the craving still lingers. You know that deep within, you are still craving the abuser, and you may even be stalking him on social media trying to keep up with his current life and the same time loathing yourself for still loving this man who is the root cause of your misery.

You may be wondering why you still love this person despite all the knowledge you gained about him and his ways of damaging innocent people.

Are you wondering why you are still in love with the abuser? Then read on to know why this is happening to you, and seek some comfort in the fact that you are *not alone* in this. A lot of victims, especially victims of abusive relationships, cannot stop loving their abusers.

One of the major reasons for this is trauma bonding. You are aware of how trauma bonding works and how it is holding you from moving on, but there are other compelling reasons as well.

You Remember Only the "Good" Times

Strange as it may seem, your brain has the innate capability to fool you into remembering only the good times that you had in the relationship. The human brain is extremely powerful, and it can trick you into constantly thinking only about the good times that you had. The good times can be few in between, but the brain remains fixated on them and plays them in a loop. You cannot stop thinking about the good times, and this can be the reason you are still in love with the abuser. Your brain constantly brings back memories from the “arousal” phase, during which the narcissist may have apologized to you, praised you for your beauty and your intelligence, or showered you with gifts. If this is the case, then it is your job to constantly remind yourself that the good times cannot and will not last because the narcissist is not a normal person.

You Remember the Narcissist’s Traumatic Past

It can be entirely possible that your narcissist ex might have experienced trauma in his life and has narrated the entire story to you in detail. The narcissist might also be dealing with his issues and past or present. This may make you feel empathy for him, and you may want to go back to help him. Remember that you did not cause the trauma, so how can you help when you have not caused it?

Abuse is always a choice, and hence, the narcissist has the choice not to be abusive, but he has chosen to be abusive, and hence, you cannot do anything to change it. Understanding his past or present trauma will not erase your trauma, and this is something that you need to remind yourself constantly.

There is nothing wrong in understanding and empathizing with others, but remember that you also deserve the same level of understanding and you must be empathetic toward yourself.

Your body and mind deserve to be treated well, and hence, focus on understanding yourself first.

Another reason this understanding of the abuser will not help is that you did not cause any of his problems, so you cannot fix it, but you can work on fixing yourself.

Savior Complex

Savior complex is a psychological phenomenon that makes people want to save those people in need. People with savior complex always want to save troubled people and help them lead better lives.

Does this definition of savior complex ring a bell? Maybe you are suffering from savior complex too?

This can be because you see the narcissist as a troubled person with his trauma, and hence, you are desperate to help him. It could also be because you were taught growing up that you must always look out for people who are suffering. There is no reason you shouldn't help people who are suffering, but the problem with people suffering from savior complex is that they show a strong tendency to help people, often sacrificing their own needs.

Is this you? If you recollect, you always served the narcissist by putting his needs above your needs, and this is why the abuse continued because if you suffer from savior complex, then you do not practice strict boundaries.

Identifying if you suffer from savior complex can help you move forward and stop loving your abuser. Savior complex has the dangerous ability to make your brain redefine the definition of nobility. It may cause you to believe that you must save people even when there is no recognition or even if you are suffering because that is noble. Saving people and not expecting anything in return is a dangerous consequence of the savior complex. This could be the reason that you want to go back to the narcissist and give him all your love yet be comfortable with all the abuse.

Seek help from a professional if you think you are suffering from savior complex.

Love Could Be a Survival Technique for You

It is possible that love for the abuser is a survival technique for you. This is because, for non abusive persons like you, it is almost impossible to understand how someone who claims to love can cause harm. Unable to understand this, you resort to denial and detach yourself from the pain and misery and continue to spend your precious time and energy trying to understand the abuser. To cope with the abuse, you subconsciously start seeing things from the abuser's point of view. This can worsen once the narcissist starts resorting to gaslighting where he can blame you for everything, and you eventually begin to agree with the abuser. Soon you learn how to appease the abuser to maintain peace. You have essentially taught your brain this survival technique, and this applies more if you are dependent on the abuser financially.

Codependency

Codependency happens when you completely become dependent on the other person, in this case, the narcissist. It is often described as relationship addiction where you become addicted to the person by focusing more and more on them and less on yourself. This becomes a vicious cycle where your thinking becomes obsessive and your behavior compulsive, leading to devastating consequences. The problem escalates where you become so obsessed with the abuser that you start justifying their abuse and abnormal behavior, doubt your perceptions, and fail to maintain healthy boundaries.

Codependency is based on deeply rooted lies within you that tell you that you are not worthy of love and respect. You believe that you are unworthy of anything good in life without even you knowing it. You feel a deep sense of shame that you cannot accept nor express. Shame is a negative feeling that leads to self-destructive behavior and negative self-evaluations, which leads to low self-esteem. Once you do not believe that you are worthy of love, you fear being rejected and judged. Your existence becomes dependent on just finding that one person who will stay with you and make you feel safe. The approval of others becomes important to you, and you cannot function when left alone. When your mood and happiness and generally existence depend on another person, you start craving that person. In this case, it is the narcissist.

A narcissist craves attention, and you crave a person who will keep coming back to you no matter what. Once the narcissist leaves you, or you leave the narcissist after identifying the damage he has done to you, after some time you start craving him back because for a very long time your existence depended on the narcissist. Now without the narcissist, you do not know how to survive.

You are ready to take care of the narcissist just so that he does leave you, so you and the narcissist are essentially two sides of the same coin.

Caretaking is also a form of control because you believe that by taking care of the person, by appeasing the other person he will not leave you. It also makes you feel in control of the situation because you feel you are controlling the other person by giving him whatever he needs, and hence, you are not vulnerable. The minute you realize that you do have him, you feel vulnerable.

Caretaking may give you a sense of purpose. If you feel you don't deserve love, you do not expect to be loved for who you are—only for what you give or do. Without your own free voice, you are considered compliant, passive, and self-effacing. You also tend to believe whatever is said to you. You crave acceptance and being wanted, need support and approval, and have a constant desire to be loved. In most cases, you believe you don't have your rights, so you instinctively go along with what you are told and put other people's needs and feelings before you, and many times, you are self-sacrificing to great lengths to please others.

All this makes you dependent on the narcissist even when you are being abused, and your needs are not being fulfilled. Being a codependent, you make it very easy for the narcissist to manipulate you, abuse you and exploit you.

Narcissists are dependent on partners, whom they can control, and you are dependent on pleasing, and hence, this is the perfect combination.

You stay or want to go back to the narcissist because of the brief periods of love and affection that the narcissist showers on you during the arousal phase. During the discard phase, you wait for the love to return and are ready to do anything for love to return.

Remember that it is all a lie. This can be extremely hard to accept, but it is the only way forward for you.

You don't have to feel shame for loving a narcissist or for having the persistent feeling to go back despite having all the knowledge.

Chapter Four: When to Start Dating Again?

After going through narcissistic abuse, the entire healing journey, and acceptance, the very thought of dating again may seem daunting.

Given that the healing journey takes forever, you may be wondering if there ever will come a time when you are ready to date again and resume life.

It is also entirely possible that you are paranoid about the thought of a romantic relationship because was it not dating that brought you in touch with the narcissist and ruined your life?

Paranoid that Everyone Is a Narcissist

It is entirely normal to feel that every person you will meet during your new dating journey may be a narcissist, and hence, you may even avoid dating completely. You may even start looking for signs of a narcissist in everyone you meet because you want to protect yourself from the trauma this time.

The fear of dating and resuming romantic relationships is one of the outcomes of narcissistic abuse. The hurt and rejection can develop a fear of intimacy in you. It can also make you not trust your judgment about people because of the gross misjudgment you made about the narcissist character. This lack of trust can prevent you from looking out for romantic relationships.

The decision to avoid can manifest itself in several forms such as denial, anger, blaming others, keeping yourself completely occupied with work and other activities, and maintaining a physical distance from people. This fear will never go away if you do not treat it.

Fear will constantly make you doubt yourself and increase anxiety leading you to believe you are not worthy of love and the cycle begins again. The best way to deal with the fear is to face it. It is important to face this fear because it drives away people who may be there to help you, protect you, and above all, give you the love you deserve.

It is also normal to lose the ability to trust in both yourself and other people. Trust will come back again naturally with the new experience and knowledge. Slowly but steadily by constantly nourishing yourself with self-care, the trust will come back in your life. The important thing to remember is that this time you are equipped with all the knowledge, and hence, trust yourself that you will be fine and that you are capable of handling anything that comes your way.

One of the best ways to build trust both in yourself and others is by ensuring that the boundaries you set are being adhered to. When you start identifying that people are respecting your boundaries, it will help you gain confidence. With increased confidence, trust also will increase.

Tips to Begin Dating

Take time to heal. Before you begin dating, it is important that you are completely healed from the abuse. It can be frustrating to watch all your friends get married or have babies, and social media does not help either. With social media, you are constantly bombarded with happy faces and happy marriages, and you might feel you are missing out on something. Desiring a happy home of your own is not a bad thing, but in order to get it right you must heal first.

Also remember, that you are now a stronger better person. Taking the time to heal is giving yourself the self-care that your body and mind needed. Hence, do not be in a rush to get done with it. Healing is a journey; enjoy the journey. It is a wonderful opportunity to get in touch with yourself and pamper yourself. This is also not a time to get into a rebound relationship. Rebounds can provide temporary relief but are never a good long-term solution. If you do not take the time to heal, the new relationship may also backfire, and you may end up in a situation like the previous one with the narcissist.

It is also bad for another reason that, if the rebound turns out to be similar to your narcissist ex, then there is a higher probability that you may again get attached to the idea of getting back to your ex. This is counterproductive and will damage you.

Hence, during the healing, the only person you have to date is you. That's right. Date yourself. Take yourself out to dinner, drinks, movies, or anything that you feel like doing. Pamper yourself and see yourself blossom. Just like you learned the art of no reaction, now is the time to learn the art of self-compassion. Train yourself that you are worthy enough of love and respect and nothing less than that.

It is during this time that you can start exercising and meditating, which are known to have a calming effect on the mind and body. Focus on physical activities to help your brain recover from the trauma.

Once you believe that you have thoroughly healed, then you can confidently begin dating. Remember that this is not a project with a definite deadline. Hence, there is no time or goal that you need to have. You will know when you are ready.

Take it slowly. Once you have decided that you have healed and have begun dating, take it extremely slow. Do not show desperation in any way to the other person. Do not allow the other person to control your life or sweep you off your feet. Spend time getting to know the person before developing intimacy and falling head over heels in love. Remember, love does not happen at first sight. If you fall too soon and become intimate, the chances are that you are getting back to your codependent self and becoming dependent on this new person for your existence. Learn to avoid that and proceed with caution. If the new person is insisting that you do things which you are uncomfortable doing or if you sense that the new person is not respecting the boundaries that you have communicated, then you must understand that it is time to move on. This is the reason it is essential that you take things slow because only then can you carefully judge the person before committing.

Learn to trust yourself. Give yourself a chance and

benefit of the doubt by beginning to trust yourself and approach dating with a clean slate. Do not let preconceived notions cloud your judgment. During the abusive relationship, you might have gotten used to rationalizing the narcissist's behavior by giving him the benefit of the doubt. This time, since you are beginning on a clean slate, do not give everyone the benefit of the doubt and let them influence you. Trust your judgment, and if you feel something is wrong, then calmly walk away.

Chapter Five: Spiritual Healing after the Narcissistic Abuse

A lot of times you must have heard that true healing happens only when you forgive and forget truly form the bottom of your heart.

You may also be wondering and thinking about the same because almost all faiths talk about forgiveness as a path to healing, but at the same time, the question arises as to how you can forgive the person who caused you so much harm and whether it is possible to forgive someone who has been responsible for your devastation, especially when they do not acknowledge what they have done.

Another question that can haunt you is whether forgiving is justified given that the narcissist is wrong on so many levels and is a dangerous person to not only you but also society in general.

You are not alone in this battle, and it is completely normal to face these questions. Do not beat yourself up for having these questions, and thinking along these lines does not make you a bad Christian at all. You might have also heard things like not forgiving will make you unspiritual.

The first thing to keep in mind is that this is *your* journey alone. You have every right to decide what to do, when to do it, and how to do it.

But it is good for you to know that forgiveness is a part of the journey. Once you have forgiven the abuser is when you truly have moved on. I struggled with forgiveness for many years until I met Diane. We connected through a support group and I was immediately drawn to her because she always spoke about her abusive partner who she still was not separated from with kindness. I wondered how someone was able to go through such cruel abuse and not only remain in the marriage but manage to keep such a positive attitude. While I do not advice anyone to remain in an abusive relationship, Diane had made her decision to stick with Tom. I couldn't understand it, but I definitely respected her position. She shared how she applied a principle of forward forgiveness, meaning that she had chosen to forgive him for the past, present and also any hurt he would inflict in the future.

This may sound shocking to you, but the truth is, it helped me to put things that had happened to me in perspective. If I was truly going to put the past behind me, I had to confront my hurt and anger, and be able to say. I forgive him forward.

Forgiveness does not mean that you have to let the abuser know that he is off and welcome him back into your life. I certainly did not do that. But like they say, un-forgiveness is like drinking poison and hoping someone else dies.

Complete forgiveness also means forgiving yourself. A lot of times despite all the healing and the steps people take or even you might have taken, you will realize that in your heart, you are not free yet. This is because while you have been able to implement no contact strictly and have established firm boundaries, you have forgotten one most important thing.

The most important thing in your self-healing journey is forgiving yourself. This is because nothing matters—no therapy sessions, no amount of self-care or pampering can do you any good—if you have truly not forgiven yourself.

Why Must You Forgive Yourself?

You must forgive yourself because of the constant blame you have gone through. A lot of times during the journey, you will be blaming yourself for allowing the narcissist to abuse you, for trusting him even after his true colors were revealed, for becoming addicted to him and seeking him out despite all the harm he has caused you. In a toxic relationship such as the one with a narcissist, the person who suffers the most is *you*. You were the harshest with yourself, and hence, you need to forgive yourself.

When you forgive truly, you are not releasing the burden of the narcissist, but you are releasing the burden you put on yourself. By forgiving yourself, you drop the baggage that you have been carrying around, so suddenly you experience freedom. Once this happens, you will realize that you are no longer haunted by the memories, and even if you recollect something from the past, they will not damage you or cause a breakdown.

Self-love and self-forgiveness are the ultimate narcissist's repellents. They work like nothing else.

Forgiveness will also remove the resentment from within that you have been holding for so long. It will cleanse your mind and body and set you free.

Forgiveness also does not mean that you have to forget everything. It is just not possible that you will completely forget everything that has happened to you. There is no way you can completely erase this chapter out of your life. And erasing your memories is not required as well. What is required is that the memories stop having a negative effect on you.

Despite healing from the trauma and even if you have forgiven the abuser, it does not mean that you must forget. Having a memory of the events will help you spot red flags in the future and help you protect yourself. During the healing process, you will eventually move from paranoia that everyone is an abuser to a normal hum being who does not have trust issues, but it always to remember the lessons that you learned, and the most important is the ability to spot red flags from a distance.

Not forgetting will also help you see how far you have come and take note of the stronger person that you are today. It will also make you a wiser person.

Last but not the least if you have survived all the abuse and have managed to heal it means that there is a protective force within you that is guiding you, and you must be proud of that.

Last but not least the entire journey of healing from a narcissist is a spiritual journey more than anything else. This is due to the fact that a spiritual journey is one where you seek reconciliation and education through enlightenment. It is the only journey which allows you to travel within you and discover your soul and mind to attain higher goals.

This journey is unique to each individual, and no journeys are going to be the same.

Healing from a narcissistic abuse forces you to go on a path of self-discovery to answer questions that arise related to anger, why you let the abuse happen, why you still love your abuser etc.

The culmination of this journey is when you have identified the answers to the questions, accepted your internal flaws, and worked on repairing them. This is the reason the healing is more a spiritual process. It is the moment of self-discovery, which will teach you that you are entitled to love and respect.

This spirituality from the narcissistic abuse comes in waves and not at a single point in time. You slowly start realizing that

- you are appreciating all the self-love and care you are giving yourself and also acknowledge that self-care is essential for leading a fulfilled life;
- it is completely fine to be a little "selfish" at

times because only when you are happy, it can you lead a happy life, and this happiness comes from within;

- you are extremely comfortable with the boundaries that you have established and no longer feel guilty for enforcing them;
- you no longer have intrusive thoughts about your narcissistic ex, and his presence also does not bother you;
- you are completely in charge of your mental and physical space and will not allow anyone to intrude into them without your permission;
- you start honoring yourself more and stop putting others needs before your needs (you no longer suffer from a savior complex);
- you completely acknowledge that a narcissist cannot be changed and that it is not your job to fix him;
- you do not break down when problems arrive; rather, you start looking for solutions on your own (this is a huge step in the right direction because this indicates that you trust

yourself and your judgment something that you would have struggled with in the initial days after the abuse).

In addition to the above, you also understand and accept that whatever happened to you was not a punishment but rather a divine lesson from God. As weird as it may sound, this is the truth. All this was essential for you to discover your true potential and accept yourself. Over time you will realize that these punishments are lessons that will help you overcome all the false beliefs that you have about yourself.

You will change from being a codependent person who also needed approval and feared rejection of a confident individual who is not dependent on anyone's approval. The narcissist will cease to have any control or power over, and no reaction will become a routine for you, not something that you need to practice carefully.

You will also realize that transformation is the only way to living your best life, and this is the key to leading your life in an emotionally fulfilling manner. This does not mean that you will never face any problems in life again or that life will be a bed of roses. This means that with the transformation that has taken place, you will be able to tackle the problems in a calm and matured manner with all the new strength that you have acquired.

Spiritual healing is the healing of your "inner spirit." It is the process of working on the life force energy within you and getting back this energy that belongs to you.

Another important learning is that from a spiritual perspective there are no victims. During the initial phase of recovery, everything seems so difficult because you consider yourself as a victim.

Considering yourself a victim will not help you grow stronger; it will rather make you weaker. This is because for centuries, society has considered victims to be weak, and victims have always been associated with weakness. You also must have grown up thinking the same. As long as you feel weak, you can never heal and move forward.

But in spirituality, there are no victims. You will come to understand this as your healing journey progresses. You will understand that each of the events that happened to you was just experiences. The abuse was also an experience that you allowed to happen at some level. You start considering the abused person as a teacher and your experience as a learning experience that taught you a lot about yourself.

You learn intuition from this experience and trust early warning signs. It is not that you would not have experienced early warning signs during the initial stages of the relationship, but you consciously decide to ignore them—you push them away and stop giving your intuition the attention that it deserves. Through the healing process, you start learning to trust your intuition again. Once you start trusting your intuition, you are no longer in a dangerous position where you will fall for a predator such as a narcissist.

You were in a dangerous situation when you were a victim. Because when you are a victim, you lack self-worth and hence attract the wrong kind of people into your life. This danger will continue forever, and there may be chances where you will move from an abusive relationship to another, and the cycle will continue.

The secret for this cycle of abuse to stop is healing from inside. The truth is though abuse happens from the outside, your inner soul gets damaged, and hence, the healing must happen inside. When you are fully empowered, you stop acting like a victim because you no longer feel like one. This automatically will prevent you from falling for abusers such as a narcissist in future because you will walk away as soon as you spot the first sign of a narcissist or any other abuser.

Spiritual healing will also help you understand that your past served a purpose in life and taught you whatever you needed to survive the future. Now that the purpose is over, the past left you, and you must be grateful for the lessons that past taught and also grateful to God that you do not have to live that fearful and traumatic life anymore. So how does one attain spiritual healing? I would say it is simply by drawing closer to God and engaging in spiritual activities like prayer, fasting, studying the bible and meditating on Gods promises. You might not feel strong enough to pray for long hours and that is not the point. What is most important is that you spend time talking to him, just like he was seating in the room with you and pouring out your heart to him.

Listening to spiritual songs also have a way of calming me personally, so on the days where I felt too overwhelmed to pray, I just played some music on my phone, over and over. The peace that comes from God is like no other, there is no way I would have made it out with my sanity intact without the help of God.

Chapter Six: Four Pillars for Recovery from Narcissistic Abuse

Now that you have learned about the healing process and how spiritual healing works, it is time to move onto the next aspect of healing.

Just like a house that has four walls, you are also made up of four walls. These four walls or pillars are what make you the person you are and help you in creating an identity for yourself.

The four pillars are as follows:

- self-esteem
- self-worth
- self-trust
- self-love

You must have noticed that throughout the book, these words have been used generously. These are the four pillars on which every human being stands. These pillars offer the support to live life, to tackle problems that life throws at you and to finally experience a fulfilled life.

Relationship with a narcissist hurts so much and causes internal damage because a narcissist methodically attacks all the four pillars. He ensures that he leaves no stone unturned in damaging every small part of all the four pillars leaving no option for you other than to fall.

To help you understand this better, imagine a storm that is raging through. Have you ever seen the destruction a storm causes and have you wondered how long it takes for the people and homes affected by the storm to reclaim their life back?

You are exactly similar to the person caught in a storm. A narcissist attacks you unannounced just like a storm when you least expect it or are least prepared. He attacks all your pillars and disturbs the foundation on which you are standing, so you fall and collapse just like those houses that fall in a storm or massive trees that get uprooted. The destruction is so much that it takes months and in some cases years for the pillars to rebuild.

There are some basic practices that you can do to help rebuild the pillars.

Self-Esteem

Self-esteem essentially means supporting yourself. It is how much control you have over yourself, your mind, your body, and your behaviors. Self-esteem is also about the perception you have about yourself and how you see yourself.

The opposite of self-esteem is self-sabotage or self-damage. During the process of healing, it is important that you build your self-esteem.

You can begin by doing simple things that will tell you that you are in control of the situation. You can start by tackling basic things such as hygiene that you might be ignoring right now because of your PTSD or depression. Something as simple as having a daily routine to take a shower or to dress decently even when at home can help you regain a sense of control. These baby steps will help you tackle the bigger problems.

Self-Worth

This is about knowing your value and respecting your worth. It is believing that you are worth the respect, love, and affection. The exact opposite of self-worth is shame and unworthiness.

After the abuse, the narcissist would have ensured that you feel a deep sense of shame and hate yourself. Self-worth is also about speaking up for your rights and standing up for yourself and what you believe in.

You need to focus on the courage to build self-worth. Courage does not mean trying to scale the mountains or running in the wild. Courage means taking measures to change your life actively. It can be applying for another job, being able to negotiate a good pay that you deserve, applying to school if you always wanted to finish school, etc. It means identifying something that you wanted to do but have never done because you believed that you were not worth it.

It also comes by not compromising on your values or doing things you are uncomfortable doing. You would have compromised on your values while trying to appease the narcissist. Once you develop courage, you will not compromise on your values and thus will develop self-worth. In my first book 'Narcissistic Abuse Recovery: A guide to finding Clarity and reclaiming your Joy after leaving a toxic relationship' I included meditation and prayers after each chapter, because I saw the need for every survivor to understand how valued and precious they are in the sight of God. Regardless of what you have come to believe about yourself, God our father has a very different view of who you are. I choose to believe that his word and it changed my life completely. I went from feeling lost, to finding hope in his promises. If you haven't read that book yet, I suggest you do. If you have tried everything else, and years after leaving your abuser you still feel stuck, angry, and broken, I suggest you start by getting a bible. Read as frequently as possible and I guarantee you would see a change in your life.

Self-Trust

Self-trust is about trusting yourself, your judgment. It means having faith in yourself and being confident about your decisions. It means not second guessing every single decision and worrying about it.

When you lack self-trust, you live in constant fear and doubt. During the relationship with the narcissist, you slowly start losing self-trust without even you realizing. It happens silently, and before you know it, you will be second-guessing everything. The narcissist achieves this by gaslighting and deflecting blame.

The only way to rebuild self-trust is to listen to your

intuition. The gut feeling that everyone talks about is what you must pay attention to. If something does not feel right to you, then trust that instinct and let it go. Gut feeling is more tangible than some more forms of intuition. Gut feeling is never wrong, as it is your inner voice trying to guide you and protect you from danger or from something that is not right for you.

Your gut feeling and intuition stop working once you start ignoring them. It is like ignoring your best friend who has nothing but the best intentions for you. Once you start ignoring your intuition and gut, they no longer guide you, and that is when you take the wrong steps.

Get it back by listening to it. Follow whatever your gut says and see the change.

Self-Love

Finally, the fourth pillar, self-love is about caring and nurturing yourself. It is about treating yourself well. Self-love takes a back seat during the relationship with a narcissist because the narcissist wants and demands all the love. When you are in a relationship with a narcissist, you cease to be in a relationship with yourself. You slowly stop loving yourself and go into self-denial and self-judgment mode. You judge yourself poorly and try to rationalize all the bad behavior being shown by the narcissist. When you do not love yourself, you go into a people-pleasing mode and develop a savior complex. By now, you know how dangerous savior complex is to your health and sanity. You start believing you are ugly and stop taking care of your health.

The medicine to this lies in loving yourself back. This can be accomplished by taking small steps such as cooking your favorite meal, eating healthy food, and eating regular meals. It could also be treating yourself at a salon or spa and just pampering yourself.

You can focus on things that you want to change about yourself and more importantly accept what you cannot change. Self-acceptance is a part of self-love because if you do not accept yourself just as you are, then there is no way that another person or the world will accept you the way you are. This is because others will treat you just as well or as bad as you treat yourself. By treating yourself well, you are teaching the world how they must treat you and conveying your boundaries and wishes to them.

How Long Does It Take to Heal Completely?

This is a question that haunts most victims because it can seem like forever with no end in sight. A lot of days you may go to bed wishing that you do not have to get up the next morning because you are afraid how bad the day will be. You will constantly feel like there is no light at the end of the tunnel.

Do not drown in this hopelessness because this kind of negative thinking will quickly take you back to victim land. The journey to victim land is a free airplane ride where you will reach the deepest levels of fear, hatred, and disgust within minutes, but remember that journey to victim land means no return.

Hence, hold onto your horses. Take comfort in the fact that God has given you this amazing opportunity to heal you, and you can start by drawing closer to him. Healing that comes from your spirit, is exactly what you need for psychological abuse, just because a lot of the scars you have are not physical ones.

There are countless women who spend their entire lives trapped in victim land and never live a happy and fulfilled life.

The truth is that there is no timeline for healing. It is not a mathematical calculation with definite results. Do not trust anyone who is telling you that it takes no more than a month or two to recover. Neither must you pay attention to fellow victims who claim to have healed in record time. You are not in competition with anyone, this is about the rest of your life, and healing needs to be thorough and deep to be sustainable.

This journey is a spiritual journey, and the destination is *you*, so it can be one month for some; it can take one year for some, and some people can take several years. Healing depends on various factors, but above all, it depends on how committed you are to the process. At times you will see no progress at all. There will also be times when from one forward stage you will take two steps back for reasons you cannot understand yourself. Despite this, persist. Persistence works magic. Keep a journal and write down everything so that when you feel demotivated, you can turn back the pages and see how far you have come.

Celebrate each milestone and make a note of it. Acknowledgment helps develop self-love and will bring you to acceptance. Again, you need to understand that you are not in competition with anyone but yourself in this and this not a race. Healing from narcissistic abuse is not like running a sprint, but it is more like a marathon. Hence, pace yourself and keep the momentum going.

It does not matter whether it takes a few months longer, but it is important that you heal completely and come out of the marathon with flying colors.

Conclusion

Congratulations. You have successfully made it to the end of the book, and this means that you have gathered all the theoretical knowledge that is required to reclaim your life back.

By this time, you may be scared and even feel like you are never going to be able to see sunshine again. That is not the aim of this book.

This book aims to help you identify the signs of narcissistic abuse and to tell yourself that *you are not crazy*. It debunks the myths that you have in your mind about yourself and to provide you with the guidance required to heal.

Narcissistic abuse is very difficult to heal from, but it is not impossible. It is difficult to heal from because narcissistic abuse is like soul rape. It affects you on at a very deep soul level and leaves you feeling violated on many levels. This way you experience emptiness because you feel like your soul has been taken away from you.

This book is to help you turn yourself back. While

you may not be able to turn back time and get back the precious hours, days, and years you spent serving the narcissist and their never-ending ego, you can most definitely turn yourself back with the help of no contact, setting firm boundaries, and finally going on a path of spiritual healing.

The only way to go forward is to take it slow. Set reasonable expectations and take each day as it comes. Do not beat yourself up if you fail to do something positive on any given day. Some days will very good and some bad. Celebrate the good days and learn from the bad days.

To completely heal from narcissistic abuse, you must be willing to dig through the dark shadows of your psyche and find out the reasons that made you stop loving yourself and start obeying the narcissist. A lot of times the quest for a soul mate stops you from doing this searching. For centuries, the concept of finding a perfect soul mate, the other half to you, has been propagated so much that you believe that is the only way to live life. When your only goal in life becomes finding a soul mate, it becomes easy to fall for a narcissist.

The goal should be to find the other half of yourself from within you and not from outside because no outsider can complete you. To be able to love some in the right manner and lead a fulfilled life, you must be whole and complete.

This journey of healing will help you find yourself and complete yourself. You will understand that you do not need anyone to complete you but that *you* are enough. Since after my divorce, I made a commitment to learn everything I could about Narcissism, and that helped me to stay strong through the trying times. It is important you give yourself the time to get to know yourself before you get to know someone else, and hence, do not jump into dating or get into a rebound relationship soon after you leave the narcissist. This might backfire and will send you back to victim land again.

Instead, you should focus on becoming your savior. Save yourself from the trauma and damage by investing in yourself. Give time to both yourself and the other person, in the case of a new relationship, before you start building your life around that person again. It is like building sand castles on the beach where the foundation is not strong. When the foundation is not strong, waves come crashing down, and the castle vanishes with no evidence left. Hence, give yourself time to get to know the other person and wait to see, till things feel right for a considerable length of time. Learn to spot red flags and walk away if you spot them.

Finally, you must stop focusing on the narcissist and your victimhood. The longer you focus on the pain and the humiliation that the narcissist caused, the longer you will be a resident of victim land. The first step to healing is to stop focusing on the negative aspects and start looking at yourself as a survivor and the past events as nothing but a bad experience. Once you start looking at the past as a bad experience, you will only retain the bad memories but not the emotions attached. Think of it as a bad dining experience. When you have a bad dining experience that left a bad taste in your mouth or caused a stomach bug, you remember not to let that happen again. Healing from abuse is just like that.

Do not let one bad experience define your life and ruin it. Instead, use that bad experience as a lesson and emerge victorious just like a phoenix.

Just like the phoenix emerges from ashes, you can rise from this experience that damaged you into a better human being after the spiritual transformation that you have undergone. I am routing for you.

References

https://www.psychologytoday.com/us/blog/inside-out/201309/the-5-stages-grieving-the-end-relationship

https://www.psychologytoday.com/us/blog/communication-success/201504/8-signs-youre-in-relationship-sexual-narcissist

http://www.thenarcissisticpersonality.com/co-parenting-narcissist/

https://thoughtcatalog.com/shahida-arabi/2018/02/this-is-what-it-really-means-to-go-no-contact-with-an-abusive-narcissist/

https://narcwise.com/2017/11/19/your-inner-magic-8-ball-name-your-values-claim-your-boundaries/

https://medium.com/@SoulGPS/10-steps-to-getting-your-life-back-after-narcissistic-abuse-96b5c74af29c

https://www.psychologytoday.com/us/blog/resolution-not-conflict/201802/parental-alienation-syndrome-what-is-it-and-who-does-it

https://www.psychologytoday.com/us/blog/anxiety-zen/201502/forget-co-parenting-narcissist-do-instead

https://www.narcissismfree.com/when-no-contact-cant-work/

https://www.loveisrespect.org/content/why-do-i-love-my-abuser/

http://www.esselmancounseling.com/2016/02/23/signs-that-youve-been-abused-by-a-narcissist/

https://hackspirit.com/3859-2/

https://medium.com/@OwnYourReality/4-pillars-for-recovery-after-narcissistic-abuse-7195a40f0b6a

https://www.narcissismfree.com/spiritual-recovery-from-emotional-abuse/

Made in the USA
Monee, IL
12 July 2020